CHARACTER

The Golden Thread In Good Living

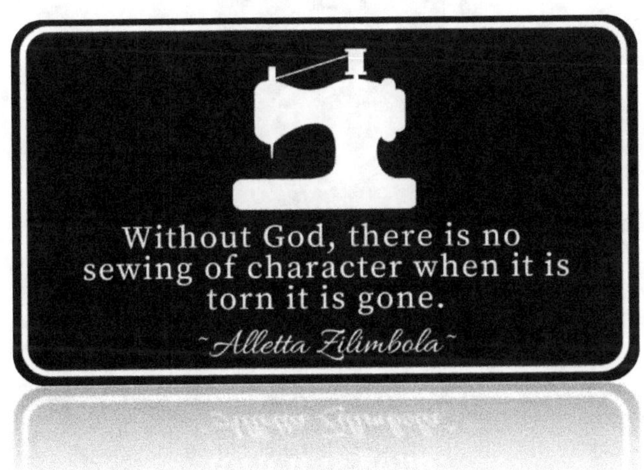

Tlhobogang Alletta Zilimbola

Published By:

Ssali Publishing House
www.salipublishing.com

The Premier Christian Publishing House in Africa

Editor: Rose Ssali
ssalirose@gmail.com
Cell +27 71 726 8717

ISBN 978-1-990901-34-8

Printed in South Africa

CHARACTER

The Sum Total of Many Traits Seasoned by God's Grace

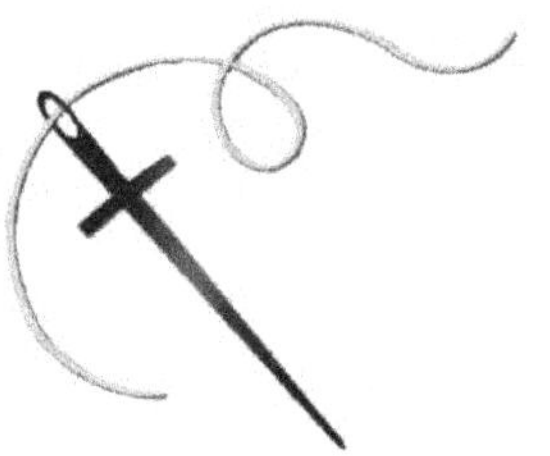

CONTENTS

ABOUT THE AUTHOR

Alletta Zilimbola is the second born child of the late Maesupeng and the granddaughter of Chief Matsime. She grew up in the village of Shiela. A born-again Christian, she and her husband, Malungelo, have brought up their three children in the fear of the Lord, highlighting the need for good character where good is defined by Scripture.

A firm believer of the fact that a lifestyle that is in keeping with Biblical principles pays the highest dividends, Alletta has written this book to inform, to teach and to encourage the Body of Christ to walk as Christ walked.

The important lesson is that in everything we do, we must exemplify Jesus Christ. He is our example of what our heavenly Father would have us do in this life. Before He ascended into heaven, Jesus told His disciples, and by extension, us, that His Father would send a helper in the person of the Holy Spirit, to guide, teach and comfort us.

Alletta lives a life of praise and worship so when she talks about gratitude and trusting in the Lord, it is from a place of knowledge and joy. She knows, beyond the shadow of a doubt, that we are a chosen generation and therefore, we have a purpose ordained for us by our heavenly Father. We must therefore invest in the things of God, acknowledge His goodness with gratitude and trust Him to guide us home to Him and there, live with Him in glory.

Characters do not change. Opinions alter, but characters are only developed.

Benjamin Disraeli

DEDICATION

This book is dedicated to my late Mom, Maesupeng Matsime, to my grandparents, Mr. Chief and Mrs Alletta Matsime.

A special dedication to my husband, Malungelo, and to our children, Lwazi, Lumka and Litha.

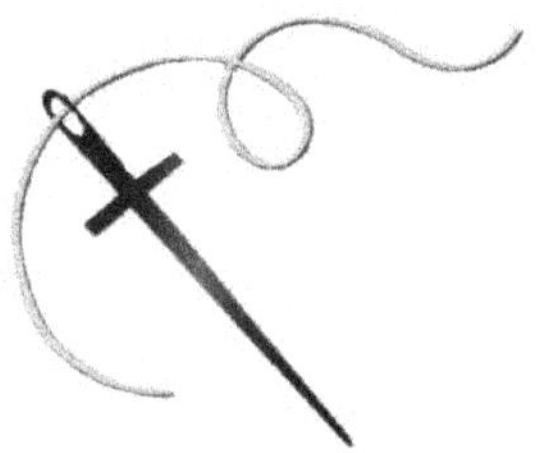

ACKNOWLEDGEMENTS

I acknowledge with gratitude the grace of our Lord Jesus Christ who loved me enough to die on the Cross that I might have eternal life.

I thank God for my husband, Malungelo Zilimbola, whose love and support is a testament of His love for God. I acknowledge our children, Lwazi, Lumka and Litha as well as our spiritual children, all of whom we love dearly in the Lord.

FOREWORD

This is an amazingly practical and well written book. Alletta Zilimbola distils the most fundamental aspects of striving towards a godly character. It is important to note that this godly character is in itself not a destination but a way of life. Excellence has no finishing line, just like Paul said, I press toward the mark of the prize of the high calling of God in Jesus Christ (Phillipians 3:14).

I have known Alletta for over two decades and I can attest that she is indeed a woman of a godly character. Alletta vowed that 2020, even with the Covid-19 crisis, was not going to be a write-off. While in lock-down she focussed on writing her book. That is character.

Together we have raised three wonderful children, Lwazi who is studying at a University in the United States of America and two boys, Lumka and Litha who are in a boarding school in the United Kingdom. We decided earlier on before we even had children, that one of us would stay at home and raise our children, in order to shape their characters from a tender age. Alletta volunteered for this role which has turned out to be a great investment in our children. The character that was built in each of the children is now sustaining them overseas.

This book was written in the context of a society where crime and corruption happen with impunity. Women and children are raped and murdered; there is widespread corruption in both the public and private sectors, and lawlessness is the order of the day. Our beloved country is crying out for men and women of good character and leaders with a godly character.

Anybody reading this book will be challenged to make better choices in life. The book seeks to sew the torn fabric of our society. The book also makes it clear that we cannot resolve our enormous challenges without the intervention of the Creator. Let's all strive toward building a nation of a godly character. Luke 2:52 says Jesus increased in wisdom and stature, and in favour with God and man. I can imagine a country populated with wise, mature and patriotic people. A nation united and in good relations with each other and God.
Stay blessed as you continue to read.

Malungelo Headman Zilimbola

THE GOLDEN THREAD

The wisdom in His Word
Is the golden thread
Which sewn into the fabric
Of our lives
Creates a beautiful character
Which dear friends
At the behest of the Holy Spirit
Will yield a pleasing aroma
For our heavenly Father
Who is generous to redeem
To sanctify
And bring us home
Into His loving care
For all eternity…

If there is character, ugliness becomes beauty; if there is none, beauty becomes ugliness.

Nigerian Proverb

INTRODUCTION

We're all living a story today. It often doesn't feel like a story. It feels like dishes in the sink. Emails in our inbox. Another round of the same old routines. Sometimes the plot is confusing and we want to cut a chapter out with sharp scissors. Sometimes we want to be the editors with the red ink. Sometimes we want to skip right to the end just to make sure it says,

"And they lived happily ever after."

There's so much we don't know, but we can be certain of this: the Author is good and we are loved. Yes, even when the unexpected sentence comes. When we face that dark-as-night period. When the syllables jumble together and we scratch our heads. Even in those places, between those lines, there is a God at work who has always been speaking, always been creating beauty out of the broken.

"Jesus also did many other things. If they were all written down, I suppose the whole world could not contain the books that would be written".
John 21:25

Your story isn't over yet. Jesus is still doing many other things. He isn't done with history. He isn't finished with the part of it that is our story either. Whatever scene we find ourselves in today, it isn't the final page.

Hold on, there is a turning coming. There is more than this, more than here and now. In addition, we are overcomers. We are warriors. We are a force to be reckoned with in this world. And whatever the future brings, our God is still holding the pen. He is the only one who gets to write "The End."

How our lives pan out is largely due to our character. Our choices determine, to a large extent, whether we have a fulfilling life or otherwise. The word fulfilling is relative. The most important thing, is that when we do come to the end, as we all will, our Lord Jesus Christ will be able to say to each one of us,

"Well done, good and faithful servant."

TAKE A BREATHER

The year 2020 has been, indisputably, one of the toughest years for many of us. Life as we knew it was thrown out of sync, our routines were disrupted and our freedoms curtailed. The ordinary became the extraordinary and questions arose that we did not seem to have answers for.

Now more than ever, it is the challenges of life that are uppermost on most people's minds. Yes, life has been, undeniably, hard lately. You do your best and some days it still feels like it's not enough. You wonder if everyone else might have it more together than you. But those are lies and here's what's true…Yes, you feel weary sometimes but you're still going strong. You get up every morning and you face a new day. You put one foot in front of the other. You don't let fear stop you. You walk through uncertainty and challenges and you don't quit.

Well, here is some good news: *you don't have to do this perfectly*. You might have moments when tears come to your eyes or the edge of your voice becomes sharper than you'd like. But this doesn't mean you're failing. It means you are a brave human fighting for what matters.

You're in a season that requires courage beyond anything that has come before. Of course you feel unsure sometimes. Of course you wonder if you have any idea what you're doing. This is what comes with conquering new territory.

Don't stop now. You're farther up the mountain than it seems. You've come so far. You will make it. You're taking one more small step today and that's enough.

And you are not alone...

"Don't be afraid, for I am with you. Don't be discouraged, for I am your God. I will strengthen you and help you. I will hold you up with my victorious right hand."
Isaiah 41:10

You are loved as you are, where you are today, and you're still climbing. It is my desire that by the time you reach the end of this book, you will have understood that you were saved by grace for a purpose. You are destined to be here right now for you and I are the chosen generation.

In that case, we must invest in the things of God, His Word, the example set by His Son, our Lord Jesus Christ. To help us do so, we have the Holy Spirit as our guide, teacher and comforter.

It is my prayer that you will be filled with gratitude because God loves us and answers our prayers. He only asks that we trust Him. If we do, His Word tells us that He will meet our every need.
Hallelujah!

When wealth is lost, nothing is lost; when health is lost, something is lost; when character is lost, all is lost.

Billy Graham

PART I

WE ARE A CHOSEN GENERATION

Character is easier kept than recovered.

Unknown

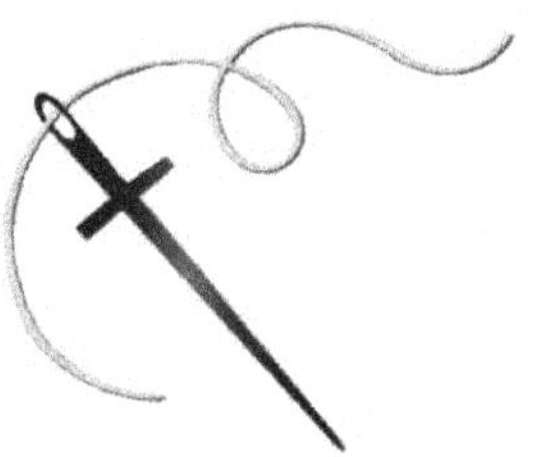

SALVATION

"For God so loved the world, that he gave his only Son, that whoever believes in him should not perish but have eternal life."
John 3:16

When thinking about salvation it's helpful to think about what we are saved from, what we are saved to, who we are saved by. It's also helpful to think about our salvation as a past, present, and future happening. Salvation is not only being saved from something it is also being saved to someone. We are saved from sin and brought to God.

The Scriptures speak of the many benefits of salvation. John 8:36 helps us see that we have been set free. We are rescued from bondage and brought into freedom. Romans 5:1 tells us that we were saved from wrath and brought into peace with God. These are only a few examples. And finally, we are saved for a relationship. God has overcome our greatest problems so that we could be brought into a relationship with Him. This is our greatest good. But how does this become ours?

Repentance and belief are really two sides of the same coin. Repentance means that we are changing our mind about God and about ourselves. We are laying down our own foolish efforts to save ourselves. We are turning away from self-sufficiency. At the same time we are turning towards Christ. We trust that He alone is the one who can save us. We are entrusting ourselves to him.

This is why the Bible says it is by grace through faith (Ephesians 2:8). Faith is simply that which links us to Christ.

The most important aspect of our repentance and faith is not its own veracity. The most important aspect of our repentance and faith is its object. When we place our faith and trust in Christ the Bible says we are saved. *"Everyone who calls on the name of the Lord will be saved,"* Joel 2:32 (also Acts 2:21 and Romans 10:13).

What is salvation? Salvation is the work of God that sets human beings in right relationship with God and with one another. It is first of all the healing of broken relationships, beginning with the healing that reconciles the Creator and the created, God and us. Our reconciliation with God leads to freedom from sin and a newness of life that is not limited by death.

HOW TO BE A MORE LOVING PERSON

The LORD has appeared of old to me, saying, 'Yes, I have loved you with an everlasting love; therefore with lovingkindness I have drawn you.
Jeremiah 31:3

Now that we live Online as much as we do Offline, we find ourselves in a culture that defines friendships and love in ways other than those we knew before the advent of the Internet.

People have been carried away by how many 'likes' they got online, how many people follow them and how large their real or perceived networks are. But love isn't about that and neither is it about the number of people we have in our lives, guests who come to our wedding (or funeral), or contacts on our phone.

God doesn't tell us how much time we're to spend with others, how many friendships we should maintain, or which social activities we must do. Instead, He describes love this way:

Love is patient and kind. Love is not jealous or boastful or proud or rude. It does not demand its own way. It is not irritable, and it keeps no record of being wronged. It

does not rejoice about in- justice but rejoices whenever the truth wins out. Love never gives up, never loses faith, is always hopeful, and endures through every circumstance.
1 Corinthians 13:4-7

None of us live this list perfectly; what I want us to see is that love is about the quality of how we treat others, not the quantity of our connections. When an expert in the law asked Jesus what it meant to love your neighbour, He replied with the parable of the Good Samaritan, a simple story about one person helping another.

Our social schedules aren't a measuring stick for our spirituality. If you want to grow in love, measure nothing. Instead, make one connection, have one conversation, show kindness to one person at a time.

The people who impress me most aren't the ones on stages or with the most likes. I'm impressed by the doctors and nurses, who have been working numerous hours, often double shifts, trying to fight against the Covid-19 pandemic.

I am impressed by the owners of some restaurants who, tirelessly, made good meals for the frontline workers, by neighbours who checked on each other and particularly on the elderly among them. They exemplified Christ.

LEARN TO SEE WITH NEW EYES

Lift up now your eyes, and look from the place where you are … for all the land which I give to you and your descendants forever… Arise, walk in the land through its length and its width, for I give it to you.

Genesis 13:15-17

*G*od told Abraham to look past where he stood into the distance, northward, *southward, eastward, and westward"* Genesis 13:14. Why? Because only what he was able to see would He be able to give him.

Faith helps us to see with new eyes. I believe our generation is suffering from spiritual blindness. Because of lack of a faith we are not able to see the things that God wants to bring into our lives. The things God has prepared for us before the foundation of the world are not always apparent to the natural eye and thus require us to tap into the realm of faith to acquire them. (Deuteronomy 29:29)

Does His Word not tell us very clearly:

"Eye has not seen, nor ear heard,
Nor have entered into the heart of man

The things which God has prepared for those who love Him. But God has revealed them to us through His Spirit. For the Spirit searches all things, yes, the deep things of God. For what man knows the things of a man except the spirit of the man which is in him? Even so no one knows the things of God except the Spirit of God. Now we have received, not the spirit of the world, but the Spirit who is from God, that we might know the things that have been freely given to us by God."
1 Corinthians 2:9-12

There are things that are not visible to the naked eye. Or instance, hydrogen and oxygen are not visible but when they combine through a chemical process they become a visible substance called water. Similarly, faith is an invisible process that allows us to respond to God's Word, producing visible effects in our lives. These are the things revealed by the Holy Spirit.

BE WISE WITH YOUR WORDS

The tongue is a small thing, but what enormous damage it can do. A great forest can be set on fire by one tiny spark. And the tongue . . . can turn our whole lives into a blazing flame of destruction and disaster.
James 3:5-6

When we lack self-control, we're vulnerable to all kinds of problems. Anything out of control in your life can harm other people and damage your close relationships. Uncontrolled anger, lust, addiction, spending, drinking, or ambition can create enormous problems.

But the greatest destroyer of relationships is an uncontrolled tongue. I read once that the average person has about 30 conversations a day. That was before the pandemic quarantine. But if it's true, that would mean we spend around one-fifth of our lives talking. At some point, your mouth will probably get you into trouble.

James compares the tongue to a tiny spark because that's all that is needed to create a great forest fire. A careless word can ignite your relationships and make them all go up in smoke.

There are words that are dangerous. Words of discouragement, disappointment, accusation, criticism, sarcasm, condemnation, or attack—the list is endless. Gossip is especially destructive because it spreads like an airborne virus. Careless words have destroyed careers, friendships, and families.

Instead of heading in a destructive direction, you can choose to use your words to build others up. Catch people doing something right and tell them about it. Affirm their character when they make difficult decisions. Lift them up with words of encouragement. Building others up with your words isn't difficult, but in our world, it is uncommon. We reflect God's glory in a dark world when we control our mouths and build others up.

FORGIVE

*Be kind and compassionate to one another, forgiving each other, just as in Christ God
forgave you.*
Ephesians 4:32

God calls us to forgive others, but how do we do that? Here are four ways to help you let go of your pain, hurt, and bitterness.

Recognize that no one is perfect. When we've been hurt, we tend to lose our perspective about the person who offended us. But we need to remember that we are all imperfect people. Colossians 3:13 says,

"Make allowance for each other's faults, and forgive anyone who offends you. Remember, the Lord forgave you, so you must forgive others."

Relinquish your right to get even. Trust God to confront the person who hurt you and trust him to work things out for you. Choose compassion over your desire to retaliate. Getting even only brings you down to the other person's level. Take the high road instead. The Bible says to treat your enemies with kindness. It's nearly impossible to do this on your own. That's why you need the love of Jesus to fill you up.

Refocus on God's plan for your life. When you are focused on the people who hurt you, you're actually letting them control your life. When you forgive them, you find the freedom to refocus on God's purpose for your life. Isaiah 26:3 says,

"You will keep in perfect peace all who trust in you, all whose thoughts are fixed on you".

Don't go another day with resentment, bitterness, and unforgiveness in your heart. Start practicing these choices and move on to live the life God created you to live.

THE POWER OF DESIRE

I want to direct your mind to what your deeply desire. What is it that you are looking for? As Jesus asked the blind man,

"What do you want me to do for you?"
Mark 10:51

Put another way, "What is the desire of your heart? How mindful, and present, are you to the longings of your heart, your deep-seated passions, or that dreamed-of destiny you imagined for yourself as a child?

Napoleon Hill wrote, *"Strong, deep rooted desire is the starting point of all achievement."* He wrote that desire is not 'hope'. It is not a wish. It is a keen, pulsating desire, which transcends everything else. He gave the analogy that a small amount of fire gives a small amount of heat. Desire is a powerful force you must learn to leverage if you are to effectively live in the identity and the authority of He who has no limits in His blessings for us.

By defining your core desire, your core value, and your core cause, you will be able to articulate the controlling idea of your story. This will, in turn, help direct your life much like the North Star provides a fixed point sailors use to maintain a ship's bearing. It is often said that desire fuels our search or the lie we prize. It is the essence of the human soul, the secret of our existence.

Delight yourself also in the Lord, And He shall give you the desires of your heart. Commit your way to the Lord, Trust also in Him, And He shall bring it to pass. He shall bring forth your righteousness as the light, And your justice as the noonday."
Psalm 37:4-6

FINISHING WELL

I have fought the good fight, I have finished the race, I have kept the faith.
Timothy 4:7

Paul says, "I have fought the good fight, I have finished the race, I have kept the faith." This well-known and oft-quoted passage is quite significant in that this epistle was Paul's last before his martyrdom in A.D. 67. It is a deeply moving affirmation of his unwavering faith and unyielding love for the gospel of Jesus Christ.

"I have fought the good fight" is also significant for believers today because it serves as a stark reminder that the Christian life is a struggle against evil—within ourselves and in the world (John 15:9; Romans 8:7; James 4:4).

Our battle is not with flesh and blood *"but against principalities, against powers, against the rulers of the darkness of this age, against spiritual hosts of wickedness in the heavenly places"* (Ephesians 6:12). The Christian life is a fight in that Christians face a never-ending struggle against evil—not an earthly military campaign, but a spiritual battle against Satan.

Paul's life and ministry provide for us a powerful example for modelling Christ today. Not only did he "fight the good fight," but he also "finished the race" and "kept the faith" (2 Timothy 4:7). Paul knew that his death was near (verse 6) but had no regrets. After Jesus took control of his life (Acts 9:15-16), Paul had lived life to the fullest, fulfilling all that Jesus had charged and empowered him to do (Ephesians 3:6; 2 Timothy 4:17). He had a remarkable sense of fulfilment and contentment with his life (Philippians 4:11-13; 1 Timothy 6:6-8).

As believers today, we can have no greater sense of fulfilment than to know, as Paul did, that we have fully accomplished all that the Lord has called us to do (Matthew 25:21). May we "fight the good fight" and "*be watchful in all things, endure afflictions, do the work of an evangelist, fulfil our ministry*" (2 Timothy 4:5).

GOD'S COMMANDMENTS ARE NOT SUGGESTIONS

Now the Lord said to Abram, 'Go from your country and your kindred and your father's house to the land that I will show you.
Genesis 12:1

When God commands us we shouldn't want Him to explain or convince us that His plans are always good. He commanded Abraham to leave his people and his place of birth and because Abraham trusted Him, he left his people and his comfort zone. We seem to act as if when God commands us, He is interested in our excuses. If He was, He would have listened to Abraham's situation. He and his wife were both old and Sarai was barren, but God spoke, and His Word does exactly what He sent it to do. God instructed Jonah to go to Nineveh but instead, Jonah ran away to Tarshish to hide from God. And we all know where he ended up.

Arise, go to Nineveh, that great city, and call out against it, for their evil has come up before me.' But Jonah rose to flee to Tarshish from the presence of the Lord. He went down to Joppa and found a ship going to Tarshish. So he paid the fare and went down into it, to go with them to Tarshish, away from the presence of the Lord.
Jonah 1:2-3

We might do well to remember that the Ten Commandments are not Ten Suggestions nor at they the Ten Requests. Even when Christ teaches about the two commandments: Love the Lord thy God with all your heart. Secondly, love your neighbour as you love yourself. Jesus, far from making a recommendation with this teaching, He is speaking of that which we must do in obedience.

BE STILL

Be still and know that I am God.
Psalm 46:10

Psalm 46:10 shows us that throughout time, people have been concerned about world events. Although the world situation as it comes to us through 24-hour news seems negative and out of control, this psalm reminds us that God is in charge of it all. In the midst of all of the turmoil, God is with us and will deliver His people.

It's one of the most famous verses in the Bible. We put it on posters, we write it in encouragement cards, we say it during times of turmoil. We long to feel this type of deep and lasting peace.

Yet if we're honest, we have trouble living it. We are rarely still, we rarely sleep without tossing and turning, and we hardly ever live sold out that God is God and we are not.

Well, then, what are we to do? How can we "cease striving" as some translations put it?

Verse 8 tells us to "Behold the works of the Lord," and it is fascinating to consider what those works might have been. We can only focus on the beauty, the might and the glory of His works if we take the time and are still. It is then that we will know that He is God.

In other words, let us not be so caught up in the hustle and bustle of life; in finding and creating our own solutions. If we look to Him, stay still and meditate on Him alone, the Creator of heaven and earth, acknowledge Him, we will surely know His presence and revel in it.

And behold, there arose a great storm on the sea, so that the boat was being swamped by the waves; but he was asleep. And they went and woke him, saying, "Save us, Lord; we are perishing." And he said to them, "Why are you afraid, O you of little faith?" Then he rose and rebuked the winds and the sea, and there was a great calm. And the men marvelled, saying, "What sort of man is this, that even winds and sea obey him?
Matthew 8:24-27

HANDLING THE STORMS OF LIFE

And behold, there arose a great storm on the sea, so that the boat was being swamped by the waves; but he was asleep. And they went and woke him, saying, "Save us, Lord; we are perishing." And he said to them, "Why are you afraid, O you of little faith?" Then he rose and rebuked the winds and the sea, and there was a great calm. And the men marvelled, saying, "What sort of man is this, that even winds and sea obey him?

Matthew 8:24-27

Jesus did not say "Let us go into the midst of the sea and drown." He said, *"Let us go over to the other side"*. But the disciples didn't trust the words of Jesus when they were caught up in a storm. This shows that the disciples still didn't comprehend Jesus' authority. They merely saw Him as a Messiah who would set them free from the tyranny of the Romans. They didn't recognize that he had authority over the wind and the waves.

The words "Let us go over to the other side" had as much authority and power as the words, *"Let there be light!"* in Genesis 1:3. They were focusing on the wind and the waves instead of the words of Christ. They were focusing on the storm instead of the fact that Jesus was in the boat.

My dear reader, we need to trust the Word of God even in the midst of a storm!

Somebody said that if you have only the Word, you will dry up; if you have only the Spirit, you will blow up. But if you have both the Word and the Spirit, you will grow up.

In addition, let me say this, prayer without the Word is like watering the ground without the seed. We need to read, meditate, and live in God's Word.

It is an amazing assessment of the validity of Holy Scripture that Peter declares it to be more dependable than a voice from heaven.

Many of us cry out to God for a word while our Bibles are lying on a shelf. God has already spoken to us through his Word!

IN HIS IMAGE

Then God said, "Let us make man in our image, after our likeness. And let them have dominion over the fish of the sea and over the birds of the heavens and over the livestock and over all the earth and over every creeping thing that creeps on the earth.
Genesis 1:26

So God created man in his own image... Which consisted both in the form of his body, and the erect stature of it, different from all other creatures; in agreement with the idea of that body, prepared in covenant for the Son of God, and which it was therein agreed he should assume in the fulness of time; and in the immortality of his soul, and in his intellectual powers, and in that purity, holiness, and righteousness in which he was created; as well as in his dominion, power, and authority over the creatures.

This, then, is the ultimate potential destiny of all mankind. It is the awe-inspiring purpose for which we were created. As Jesus quoted, foreseeing our destiny reached, *"I said, 'You are gods.'"* Let us all, then, be ever thankful. For it can't get any higher than that.

In addition, Jesus said that we would do greater things than He did, what this means is that we will spiritually raise people from the dead to give them eternal life, which is to know the only true God and Jesus Christ whom He has sent.

It is a shame that some people have mistaken being average for being humble, as God's Will for humanity. A mindset of mediocrity fails to recognize that God created human beings in His image as representatives of His excellence and glory (Isaiah 43:7)

When we put our greatness on display, we glorify God as the light and salt of the earth (Matthew 5:13-16). Our potential in the Kingdom is limitless. Whatever we focus on and truly desire, with God's help we can achieve (Philippians 4:13).

WHO ARE YOU WALKING WITH?

Now when Abram was ninety-nine years old, the Lord appeared to Abram and said to him,
"I am God Almighty;
Walk before Me, and be blameless.
Genesis 17:1

'He walked with God.' That is all. There is no need to tell what he did or tried to do, how he sorrowed or joyed, what were his circumstances. These may all fade from men's knowledge as they have somewhat faded from his memory up yonder. It is enough that he walked with God.

Of course, we have here, underlying the phrase, the familiar comparison of life to a journey, with all its suggestions of constant change and constant effort, and with the suggestion, too, that each life should be a progress directly tending to one clearly recognised goal. But passing from that, let us just think for a moment of the characteristics which must go to make up a life of which we can say that is one walking with God. The first of these is clearly the one that the writer of the Epistle to the Hebrews puts his finger upon, when he makes faith the spring of Enoch's career.

When you walk with someone you obviously won't be going in opposite directions. If you walk in a different direction you can't listen to them, you can't enjoy them, you can't share things with them, and you won't be able to understand them. When you walk with the Lord, your will is going to align with His will. Since you're walking side by side with Him your focus will be on Him.

When you're constantly walking with someone you're going to understand them better than you ever did. You're going to know their heart. Walking with God is not just a time in the prayer closet, it's a lifestyle that we can only obtain through Jesus Christ. When you walk with God you choose to imitate Him and glorify Him in every way.

AND THE LORD REMEMBERED HER

*They rose early in the morning and worshiped before the Lord … And Elkanah
knew Hannah his wife, and the Lord remembered her.*
1 Samuel 1:19

From a place of deep sadness Hannah prays to God, vowing that if God will give her a son, she will dedicate that son to God. And God answers! Obviously, this is not always the case: there is no simple formula that if we want something enough and pray for it hard enough, God will give it. But God answers Hannah, and she responds with a prayer extolling God's power to reverse people's situations.

Hannah responds to everything in a prayer that begins and ends with the affirmation that human strength comes from and is exalted in God. God is incomparable; there is no other like this God, who knows and also weighs actions (1 Samuel 2:2-3). The heart of Hannah's prayer (1 Samuel 2:4-8) affirms that God makes surprising reversals: the strong become weak and the weak become strong.

However, the purpose of prayer is not to solve all our problems so that we can live happy, trouble-free, self-centred lives. The purpose of prayer is to get God's Will done, to glorify Him.

Hannah knew that God's purpose for His people superseded her personal desire for a son. So, while she prayed for a son, she also prayed for God's greater purpose and willingly yielded her son to meet that purpose. That's how God wants us to pray—not just to meet our needs, but for His purpose to be fulfilled through the answers to our prayers.

God is still looking for men and women like Hannah: People with problems, who will take their problems to God in prayer according to His purpose so that He gets the praise.

HIS GRACE IS SUFFICIENT

But he said to me, "My grace is sufficient for you, for my power is made perfect in weakness." Therefore I will boast all the more gladly about my weaknesses, so that Christ's power may rest on me.
2 Corinthians 12:9

There's a saying among seismologists: "Earthquakes don't kill people. Buildings kill people."

It's not the enormous shock waves that cause most injuries and fatalities. It's how the structures in which people live, work, and congregate react to those shock waves that literally spell the difference between life and death. While all buildings can, figuratively, carry their own weight, they are not generally designed to resist the irregular movement produced by an earthquake, which causes the building structure and foundation to crumble and come tumbling down.

Such destruction also occurs on a spiritual level as well, especially when unexpected events change our spiritual landscape. These occur when life takes an unexpected and cruel twist that rocks our nicely built world.

The good news is that the power of God's grace and love are more than sufficient to help us survive these spiritual earthquakes no matter what they may be.

In his second letter to the Corinthian church, Apostle Paul looks at the sufficiency of God and sees that no spiritual earthquake is so devastating, or so intense, that God is not capable of overcoming it.

Paul reveals this reality in his own life as the Lord made it clear that His grace was sufficient for whatever difficulty, trial, or tribulation Paul was experiencing.

Paul knew that His grace is sufficient. Do we?

You shall not bow down to them or serve them, for I the Lord your God am a jealous God, visiting the iniquity of the fathers on the children to the third and the fourth generation of those who hate me.
Exodus 20:5

YOU SHALL HAVE NO OTHER GODS BEFORE ME

You shall not bow down to them or serve them, for I the Lord your God am a jealous God, visiting the iniquity of the fathers on the children to the third and the fourth generation of those who hate me.
Exodus 20:5

Not only inward reverence is forbidden, but also all outward gestures that naturally or customarily express reverence, whether bowing down the body, or bending the knee, or kissing the idol, or one's hand towards it.

Nor serve them; or, worship them, either inwardly in thy mind, or outwardly by any sensible mean or sign of worship given to them, as incense or sacrifice, vowing to them, or swearing by them, or the like. A jealous God, He is impatient of any partner in thy love and worship, and full of wrath against them that give my glory to images.

Visiting the iniquity of the fathers upon the children: It is a fact that, under God's natural government of the world, the iniquity of fathers is visited upon their children. Diseases caused by vicious courses are transmitted. The parents' extravagance leaves their children beggars. To be the son of a felon is to be heavily handicapped in the race of life. That this should be so is perhaps involved in "the nature of things"—at any rate, it is part of the scheme of Divine government by which the world is ordered. We all inherit countless disadvantages on account of our first parents' sin.

The knowledge that their sins will put their children at a disadvantage is calculated to check men in their evil courses more than almost anything else; and this check could not be removed without a sensible diminution of the restraints which withhold men from vice. Still, the penalty upon the children is not final or irreversible. It is needless to say that, as respects another world, their parents' iniquities will not be visited on them.

PART II

INVEST IN THE THINGS OF GOD

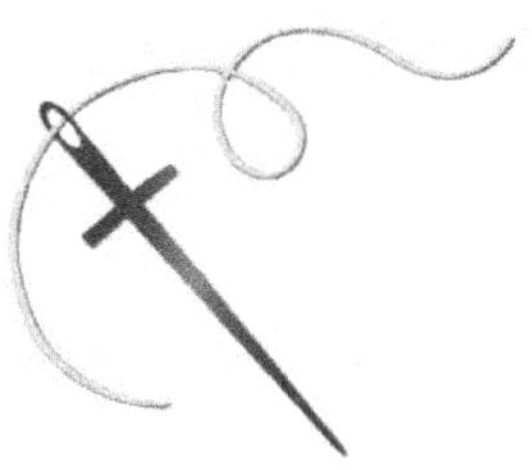

I have more understanding than all my teachers, for your testimonies are my meditation.

Psalms 119:99

Wherever man goes to dwell his character goes with him.

African Proverb

HE ORDERS MY STEPS

The Lord directs the steps of the godly. He delights in every detail of their lives.
Psalm 37:23

Man was given intelligence, Lions were given their roar, Elephants were given their size and Cheetahs were given their speed. God gave us a brain to use for His glory and yet, many of us are damaging it with substances rather than using it. We should be studying His Word to figure out what He promised. We don't know what is being promised and that is why we are doing everything He said we shouldn't do.

I have more understanding than all my teachers: It is no reflection upon my teachers, but rather an honour to them, for me to improve so as to excel them, and no longer to need them. By meditation we preach to ourselves, and so we come to understand more than our teachers, for we come to understand our hearts, which they cannot.

Herein, too, God wonderfully shows His glory, that, whosoever be the instrument, He is the dispenser of light and glory, giving more by the instrument than it has in itself. It is right to plan. However, we need to do it with the necessary humility, recognising that our plans will only succeed *'if it is the Lord's will'* (see James 4:13–15). The writer of Proverbs says, *'In your heart you may plan your course, but the Lord determines your steps'* (Proverbs 16:9).

Sometimes we align our plans with God's purposes. At other times –
certainly in my experience – God overrules our plans. We should always
bear in mind that we may have got it wrong and that, ultimately,
thankfully, it is the Lord who determines our steps.

STRENGTHEN YOURSELF IN THE LORD

This kind can only come out by nothing but prayer and fasting.
Mark 9:29

A man brought his son to Jesus. The young boy was prone to seizures which were attributed to being possessed by demons. Jesus' disciples had been unable to cast out the evil spirits. When Jesus successfully cast out the evil spirits, his disciples asked Him why they had not been able to do the same. He told them that some things were only possible by prayer and fasting.

I believe it goes without saying that if we are facing any challenge, we have tried anything and nothing is working, perhaps it is a situation, circumstance or person who can only be sorted out and you restored by nothing but prayer and supplication.

We must realize that if we fall short in our pursuit of a miracle, the lack is never on God's side of the equation. Most of us fast and pray for a specific miracle. May I suggest that instead, we pursue a miracle lifestyle.

You see, Jesus did not fast nor pray before casting the evil spirits out of the young boy. His life was filled with prayer and fasting which gave Him access to the desired supernatural way of living.

Why is it important to get this right? Is it only so that you resolve all issues that you encounter? No, we do it because we have better quality of life, emotionally, spiritually and yes, physically. Even more so, once this is our lifestyle, our lives are a heavenly demonstration. This is one of the ways that draws people to Christ.

LIGHT AND DARKNESS

Again Jesus spoke to them, saying, "I am the light of the world. Whoever follows me will not walk in darkness, but will have the light of life.
John 8:12

Darkness can be very scary and lots of things happen in the dark. The only thing that is not scared of the dark is light. When light shows up, darkness surrenders by disappearing then the light can rule. When we are in the light, we can see where we are going. Some people are able to lighten up other people's lives, but don't rely on anybody's light in case they don't come back to light up your path. God can lighten up your path at no cost, make Him your Saviour then your path will be lit up.

The Light Directs:

Anyone who gets up in the middle of the night understands the necessity of turning on a light. When the children of Israel where in the wilderness, God uses light to guide their path - *"The Lord went ahead of them. He guided them during the day with a pillar of cloud, and he provided light at night with a pillar of fire. This allowed them to travel by day or by night."* Exodus 13:21; Nehemiah 9:2

When darkness looms in our lives, we can either sit in the dark and bemoan our circumstances or we can seek the light. Upon finding the light, it is imperative that we learn about the source of light.

Light is used to symbolize God, faith, and holiness throughout Scripture. As Christians, we are called to not only walk in the light but to be the light for others. When you repent and put your trust in Christ alone for salvation you will be a light. Not only do you see everything more clearly, but the light will come to live inside of you. The light of the gospel will transform you.

A LOOK IN THE MIRROR

But we all, with unveiled face, beholding as in a mirror the glory of the Lord, are being transformed into the same image from glory to glory, just as by the Spirit of the Lord.
2 Corinthians 3:18

Are you looking at your weakness? When you look into the mirror who do you see? Paul tells us in 2 Corinthians 3:18 (NKJV) "we all, with unveiled face, beholding as in a mirror the glory of the Lord, are being transformed into the same image from glory to glory, just as by the Spirit of the Lord."

It says WE are the glory of the Lord. In Jesus we are a chosen generation, part of a royal priesthood and the glory of the Lord, and the King has offered us a place at His table! We are heirs of His great throne!!

In Him, we should have a victor mentality! Press forward — know who you are in Him and take your rightful seat at the King's Table. However, we can only know who He is, and therefore who we are in Him, if we are students of the Word. By delving in it we will have the constant reminder of who we are. The Bible is the mirror we should be looking into, not the world's reflection of who we are.

What we see in the mirror is not the Law but the Lord. In fact we are transformed by beholding the glory of the Lord.

James writes that the mirror does not show you what is wrong with you. Read carefully, James tells us it is when we leave the mirror, we do what is wrong. He says this is due to the fact that we forgot how we look like. In other words we do the wrong because we forgot who we are, not what we should do.

So go ahead… have a good look at the mirror. Take a good look at Jesus. That is how you look like now.

"The one who gives an answer before he listens—this is foolishness and disgrace for him."
Proverbs 18:13

One of the problems with humans is that we like to fix things. When we see a problem, we want to quickly jump to how we can solve it so we can move on. But God wants you to be a feeler before you're a fixer. He wants you to feel someone's pain before you try to solve the problem.

You may be barely into a conversation before you think, "I know how to fix this." But that's not loving. People don't care what you know until they know that you care. They want to feel heard. They want to feel loved. They want to feel understood. There is healing in sharing. Your ear is a healing tool God can use if you'll learn to listen without trying to fix anything.

When Jesus hears that his friend Lazarus is sick, he takes three days to travel what should have taken less than a day. By the time Jesus arrives, Lazarus is dead. His sisters are grieving and tell Jesus that, if he had come sooner, Lazarus would not have died.

Jesus' delay might seem callous, but He has a plan: He doesn't want to heal Lazarus. He wants to raise him from the dead to show He, Jesus, is the Son of God. He already knew the solution before Lazarus even got sick.

"Jesus saw her weeping, and he saw how the people with her were weeping also; his heart was touched, and he was deeply moved. 'Where have you buried him?' he asked them. 'Come and see, Lord,' they answered. Jesus wept".
John 11:33-35

Jesus is not unconcerned about their pain. When He sees everybody around Him grieving, He mirrors it. He enters into it. Jesus knows the solution, but it doesn't keep Him from sharing their grief. He shares their feelings, not His solution.

You may know the solution, but you need to hold off. If you're going to be a great listener, you've got to listen to someone's feelings and enter into that person's pain.

The ability to listen is a great character trait worth developing. There is truth the adage that people do not care about what you know until they know that you care.

As in water face reflects face, so the heart of man reflects the man.

Proverbs 27:19

THE ASSURANCE OF A BOUNTIFUL HARVEST

Now he who supplies seed to the sower and bread for food will also supply and increase your store of seed and will enlarge the harvest of your righteousness.
2 Corinthians 9:10

Everyone in this world depends wholly upon the goodness of God, whether they believe in Him or not.

Paul's subject in 2 Corinthians 9:10, however, is not food or agriculture, but gifts. When a Christian gives, he does not depend on his own resources, but on God's goodness. God, the great provider, is using that Christian to show His (God's) goodness in the world. So, God himself provides what that Christian gives. That is like the farmer's supply of seed. Although it may seem small, God uses it to provide for people in a wonderful way. The seed may be small but the harvest is plentiful. So a gift that seems small can, by the power of God, achieve great results.

Paul compares those results to the fruits of the harvest. The natural harvest astonishes us because it is so plentiful. In the same manner, the results of a person's good and generous acts can astonish us. A farmer works hard for his harvest, but that harvest depends completely on the

goodness of God. So, a person may work hard for the money to give -
but the results of that gift are the work of God.

So, the promise that Paul makes in 2 Corinthians 9:10 encourages us.
God, the great provider, does not just provide seed and food. He also
provides for us, so that we can give for His work. In addition, He uses
those gifts to bring about results that last.

THE VALUE OF TIME

*Be careful how you live. Don't live like fools, but like those who are wise. Make the
most of every opportunity in these evil days.*
Ephesians 5:15-16

Time is your most precious commodity. You only have a limited amount of it. It's estimated that people will live an average of 72 years, or 26,000 days. You may think you've got plenty of days left, but, if you're over 27, you've already passed 10,000 days. You're not getting any of those days back, and that's what makes time your most precious resource.

You can always get more money. You can always get more energy. But you cannot create more time. You have a certain number of days in your life, and that's it. When you spend them, they're gone. So life management is really time management. If you learn to manage your time, then you learn to manage your life.

The opposite of careful is careless. The Bible tells you not to be careless with your life. Be careful. That means you should be intentional and deliberate with your time.

Do you know what it looks like to be careless with your time? On average, people spend three hours and 15 minutes on their phone a day.

But being careful with your time means being aware of how you spend it and of whether you are spending it on things that really matter.

It's not a sin for you to spend five hours watching cute videos on YouTube or chatting with friends online, but it might not be the best use of your time. Some things aren't necessarily wrong. They're just not necessary. It may not be wrong, but is it worth giving your life for?

GREAT COMMUNICATION STARTS WITH LOVE

If I could speak all the languages of earth and of angels, but didn't love others, I would only be a noisy gong or a clanging cymbal.
1 Corinthians 13:1

Love is the character trait that best explains and demonstrates who Christ is. Therefore, if we are to exemplify Him, whoever you're going to have a conversation with—a child, a spouse, a friend, an ex, or a colleague —we must look at that person with eyes of love.

Words without love are just noise. If we don't speak in love, it doesn't matter what the conversation is about or how eloquent we are. We will have wasted our breath.

How do you communicate love in a conversation? For one thing, you communicate love with your eyes, the way you look at somebody. Have you ever looked at somebody and known that person wasn't loving you at that moment? Or have you ever looked at somebody and, without the other person saying a word, known that person loved you?

Your eyes are powerful tools for showing love. Start your conversations with your eyes. Use your eyes to give people your attention, because attention is love. When you pay attention to people, you're saying you love them. If you don't give them your attention, you'll never have a productive conversation or build stronger relationships.

Jesus modelled this. When a young man came to Him one day with a question, here's how He responded:

"Jesus felt genuine love for this man as he looked at him."
Mark 10:21

Jesus looked, and He loved.

ARE YOU LIVING BY FAITH OR BY FEAR?

By faith (Moses) left Egypt, not fearing the king's anger; he persevered because he saw him who is invisible.
Hebrews 11:27

Moses teaches us that living by faith rather than by fear is a choice. He went to the most powerful man in the world, at the time, and said,

"You know those slaves that are building all your pyramids? I'm taking them, and we're all leaving. You're not going to have slave labour anymore. Let my people go."

Moses had every reason to be afraid. He was going up against a powerful man who was considered a god, and whatever Pharaoh said, you had to do. What he said was the law. And here came Moses and declared,

"We aren't going to do what you say anymore. I'm not afraid of you because I report to a higher authority." That took some courage!

I cannot overemphasize the importance of faith for the rest of your life. The Bible says that whatever is not of faith is sin. How many times did you sin this week? A lot. So did I. Because anything I did that wasn't done in faith but was done in doubt was a sin. The Bible also says that without faith it is impossible to please God.

Do you want something to change in your life? Instead of complaining, start believing. God is not moved by complaints. God is moved by faith, a truth we see in these words of Jesus:

"According to your faith let it be done to you".
Matthew 9:29.

You get to choose what he does in your life. Here's the key: What matters is not the size of your faith but the size of the God you put it in. A little faith in a big God gets big results!

PART III

LET THE HOLY SPIRIT GUIDE YOU

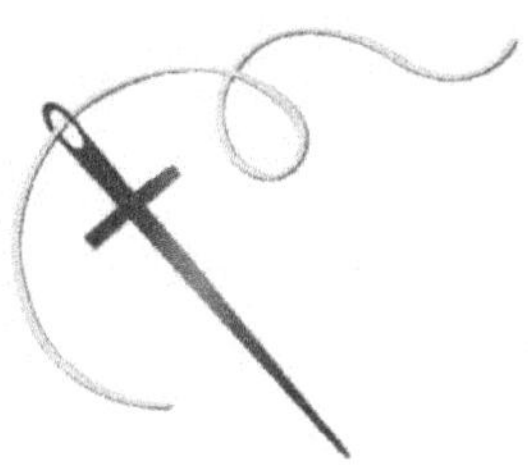

Search me, God, and know my heart; test me and know my anxious thoughts. See if there is any offensive way in me, and lead me in the way everlasting.

Psalm 139:23-24

If there is righteousness in the heart, there will be beauty in character. If there is beauty in character, there will be harmony in the home. If there is harmony in the home, there will be order in the nation.

Chinese Proverb

CHARACTER IN TIMES OF CONFLICT

Brothers and sisters, do not slander one another. Anyone who speaks against a brother or sister or judges them speaks against the law and judges it. When you judge the law, you are not keeping it, but sitting judgment of it.
James 4:11-12

We encounter conflict all the time, whether at home, at school and the workplace. We certainly read and are confronted with conflict in the media all the time. What character traits do we need in order to manage conflict well? Can those around us see Christ exemplified in our conduct?

One of the best strategies for de-escalating conflict is also one of the scariest things you can do: Asking God to give you a clear picture of yourself.

Search me, God, and know my heart; test me and know my anxious thoughts. See if there is any offensive way in me, and lead me in the way everlasting.
Psalm 139:23-24

When you're in conflict, you bring all kinds of emotions and misconceptions to the table. Your responsibility is to ask God to point out your own shortcomings—not the shortcomings of your spouse, your kid, your colleague, your friend, or your neighbour. Consider asking God to make clear to you anything in you that is wrong and then lead you on the path that is always right.

When you genuinely pray those verses from Psalm 139, God will show you the right way. He's not going to play games with you, and He always forgives—even when He points out that part of the problem in the conflict is you.

An attitude of humility and seeking to walk as Christ did will help you and I resolve many a conflict and reduce the opportunity for many more. As God reveals to you the sin in your life, you must take responsibility for it. And that may mean you need to bring it up in conversation with the other person. It always means you get right with God. Your job is to admit any part of the conflict that was caused by your bias, insensitivity, immaturity, or negligence—or any other reason.

Jesus made this point in the Sermon on the Mount. He says in Matthew 7:3-5,

"And why worry about a speck in the eye of a brother when you have a board in your own? Should you say, 'Friend, let me help you get that speck out of your eye,' when you can't even see because of the board in your own? Hypocrite! First get rid of the board. Then you can see to help your brother".

Pointing the finger will never resolve conflict. You must first look at yourself and ask God for wisdom to recognize your sin and take responsibility for it. It will never be easy, but it will always be the right choice.

PATIENCE IS, INDEED, A VIRTUE

We count as blessed those who have persevered.
James 5:11

When you are patient, it builds your character, you avoid mistakes, and you're going to reach your goals. When you're patient, you're going to be honoured by others and have happier relationships. There are all kinds of blessings and benefits.

Have you noticed—especially during this time of the coronavirus—that it's hard to be patient when you're tired? We're all feeling weary from the drawn-out uncertainty and craziness of the pandemic. However,

"Let us not get tired of doing what is right, for after a while we will reap a harvest of blessing if we don't get discouraged and give up".
Galatians 6:9

Jesus says in Matthew 5:11-12,

"Blessed are you when people insult you, persecute you and falsely say all kinds of evil against you because of me. Rejoice and be glad, because great is your reward in heaven".

When someone hurts you, one of your strongest desires may be to retaliate. People have experienced a lot of hurt feelings lately when it comes to how we choose to respond to the pandemic. And with that comes a lot of temptation to fight back and lash out. You're most like Jesus when you refuse to fight back.

Even when He was accused and mistreated, Jesus chose to do what was right and not retaliate in the middle of a crisis. If you choose to let God handle it when someone hurts you, He sees it. And He will bless you.

THE GRACE TO BE HUMBLE

Only someone too stupid to find his way home would wear himself out with work.
Ecclesiastes 10:15

We don't have all the answers. We can't do everything. If we're struggling to find balance in our lives, those admissions can transform everything.

Maria was the personal assistant to Mark, the CEO of a major corporation. His work ethic was unparalleled. However, Maria always persuaded him to balance his work life with his social life. Many a time, she picked the children from school, attended their parent-teacher meetings and even sat with them at the doctors' clinics.

One day, Mark fell asleep on the wheel while driving home after a 12-hour day at work. His car rolled twice before coming to a stop. By God's grace, he survived with minor injuries. In that split second when he thought he was going to die, Mark remembered Maria's words which he now interpreted to say,

"You are not God. It's foolish to wear yourself out with work. It's a way of saying that it all depends on you, that everything will crash down if you don't keep the world spinning. That's just not true! You're not the general manager of the universe. The universe will not fall apart if you take time to rest, if you take time to balance your life. God has it under control."

Often we do this to ourselves because we're trying to please everyone. Learn this lesson today: You can't please everyone. Even God can't please everyone! One person wants it to rain. Another one wants it to be sunny. It's absurd to try doing what even God can't do.

When you live for the expectations of others, you pile a ton of "shoulds" on your shoulders. You may think, "I should work more hours," "I should be as active as all the other parents," or "I should volunteer for this project." But realize this: No one is forcing you to do those things. Overworking is your choice. You choose to take on the extra work or not to take it on. And you choose the consequences that come with your choice.

When you deny your humanity and try to do it all, you're robbing God of His glory. The Bible declares this in 2 Corinthians 4:7:

"We have this treasure in jars of clay to show that this all-surpassing power is from God and not from us".

Paul reminds us that we're human beings. We're feeble and fragile. Jars of clay break easily. If you drop them, they shatter. Clay pots have to be handled appropriately and with care. If not, they'll be destroyed.

But the good news is that through our feebleness, the power and glory of God shine through. Your humanity isn't something to hide. Instead, you can celebrate the power of God working through your limitations.
So admit it: You're human. Thank God for that!

WHAT YOU NEED TO KNOW AND WHERE YOU NEED TO GO

When the Spirit of truth comes, he will lead you into all truth.
John 16:13

Before Jesus ascended to heaven, He promised his followers He'd send a helper, the Holy Spirit. This helper would always stay with God's people—and that includes you and me!

The Holy Spirit fulfils many roles, including telling you what you need to know and revealing where you need to go.

The Holy Spirit teaches you a lot of the big things that you need to know in life—like letting you know what's true and what's not.

He also gives you insight moment by moment. As you learn to let the Spirit lead you, He tells you what you need to know just as you need it.

Have you ever read a Bible verse one morning and then, a few hours later, recalled that verse at a moment when you really needed it? That was the Holy Spirit.

Sometimes God does this for your benefit. But sometimes He does it for someone else's benefit. God lets you share the truth He's shown you. God's Spirit will also help you get where you need to go.

Has God put a dream in your heart that you could never achieve on your own? If you let the Holy Spirit guide you, you will go to places you never imagined.

The Bible is full of examples of people who followed God's guidance. Luke 2:27 says,

"The Spirit led Simeon to the Temple".

When Simeon arrived at the temple that day, he had the highest privilege: He dedicated the baby Jesus to God.

In the book of Acts we encounter the story of another person who obeyed God's Spirit. A man named Philip was walking down a dusty road one day when an Ethiopian leader rode by in a chariot. Acts 8:29 says,

"The Spirit said to Philip, 'Go over and join this chariot'".

Philip obeyed the Spirit and found the man reading in the book of Isaiah about the Messiah. Philip told him that the Messiah had come. The man immediately asked to be baptized, and he took Christianity with him back to Ethiopia.

Because Philip listened to the Holy Spirit's nudge, he got to be part of God's work. When you listen to God's Spirit, He'll let you in on his work, too.

When you listen and follow the Holy Spirit's direction, you'll find your faith increasing because you'll consistently see God at work in your life. You'll learn you can count on Him to tell you what you need to know and show you where you need to go.

Be anxious for nothing, but in everything by prayer and supplication,
with thanksgiving, let your requests be made known to God.

Philippians 4:6

WHEN YOUR PLANS AND GOD'S PLANS DON'T MATCH

My thoughts are not like your thoughts. Your ways are not like my ways.
Isaiah 55:8

Life is full of interruptions. Sometimes we have big plans—for a career, family, or ministry—but God takes our lives in a different direction. When our plans and God's plans don't match up, we often try to kick down the door. Then things get worse.

Just ask Jonah. He learned the hard way how to respond when God's plans and his plans didn't match. God told Jonah to warn the people of Nineveh that they needed to repent from their evil ways. But Jonah ran from God and ended up in the belly of a big fish, so God had to rescue him.

Jonah then did what God had said to do, but when the people of Nineveh repented and God didn't punish them, the prophet was extremely disappointed. So God gave Jonah an object lesson. God caused a plant to grow large enough to give Jonah shade. Then he sent a worm to attack the plant and kill it. The next day, as the sun beat down on Jonah's head, he expressed his frustration to God. And that's when

God reminded Jonah of four truths to remember when God's plans differ from ours.

God can see things you can't. He can see the past and the present and the future all at the same time. He created time, so He is not subject to time.

God is good to you even when you're cranky. You may have been going the opposite direction from God, and He still covers you with shade. God cares about your comfort because that's the kind of God He is. He loves you even when you're unlovable.

God is in control of every detail of your life. Your plans don't fail randomly. God has a purpose in everything in your life. Jonah shows us that God uses both the big (a large fish) and the small (a worm) to direct our lives, but He is in control of it all.

God wants you to focus on what will last. Most of what worries you won't be around tomorrow. God wanted Jonah to care about the salvation of the people of Nineveh, not a plant that would die the next day. Above all else, focus on getting God's Word into your heart and bringing people into His family.

Just because your plans aren't turning out the way you want doesn't mean God isn't intimately involved in every step. Ask God to help you see His hand in your broken plans, and trust Him in His goodness as He shows you the way forward.

Character is not what he had, or even what he does which expresses the worth of a man, but what he is.

Henri Frederic Amiel

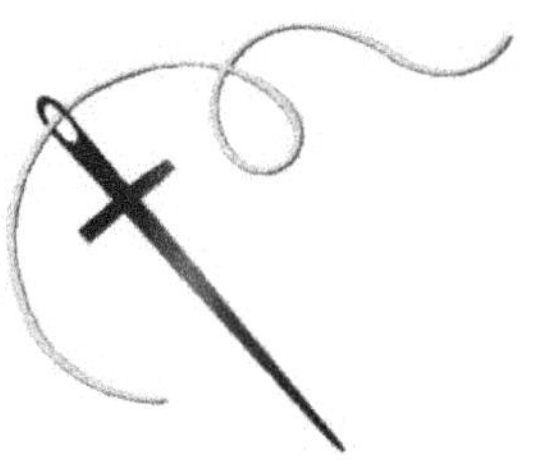

PART IV

In Everything Give Thanks

Action, looks, words, steps, form the alphabet by which you may spell character.

Johann Kaspar Lavater

THANKING GOD IN ADVANCE

I will sacrifice to you with songs of thanksgiving. I will keep my vow. Victory belongs to the LORD!
Jonah 2:9

When you feel hopeless, it seems counterproductive to express gratitude. Why would you feel grateful when you've hit rock bottom?

Just ask Jonah. At the end of his prayer from the belly of the big fish, before God rescued him, he shows us how to thank God in advance for answering our prayers:

"I will sacrifice to you with songs of thanksgiving. I will keep my vow. Victory belongs to the Lord!"
Jonah 2:9

What's the difference between gratitude before and gratitude after? If I wait to thank God until after he answers my prayer, that's gratitude. But if I thank God in advance, before he answers my prayer, that's faith. We always want to thank God when he answers our prayers, but we show faith in God if we also do it beforehand.

How do you thank God in advance? Jonah shows us three ways:

Jonah thanked God by praising him. In Hebrews 13:15, we're told,

"Through Jesus, therefore, let us continually offer to God a sacrifice of praise—the fruit of lips that confess his name".

Jonah thanked God by returning to his mission. Jonah knew he messed up. We've all been there, yet that doesn't stop God's mission for you. Jonah's life mission remained the same. Your life mission remains the same too, even when you mess up.

Jonah thanked God by trusting Him for success. Proverbs 3:5-6 teaches, *"Trust in the LORD with all your heart; do not depend on your own understanding. Seek his will in all you do, and he will show you which path to take".*

In Jonah 1, we see Jonah running from God. In Jonah 2, we see Jonah running to God and His grace. In the next chapter, we'll see Jonah running with God.

God will never abandon you, even if you disobey His will. That's why you can thank Him even before your prayers are answered.

GRATITUDE

I will give thanks to you, Lord, with all my heart; I will tell of all your wonderful deeds.
Psalm 9:1

We have so much to be grateful for in this life. Each and every day. But reality is that sometimes constant life demands, struggles, and worries give more room to defeat than to a heart of thanks. Or we forget, in the midst of busyness and pressures, just to pause and give thanks, for all that God has done, and continues to do in our lives.

Sometimes it really is a sacrifice to offer praise and thanks. We may not feel like it. We're struggling. We're weary. Or maybe, we feel like He let us down. We think God seems distant, like He's far away, or doesn't really care about what's troubling us. Painful life blows and losses might have recently sent us spiralling.

But here's what can make a lasting difference. We have a choice, every day, to give Him thanks. And with a heart of thanksgiving, we realize that no matter what we face, God doesn't just work to change our situations and help us through our problems. He does more. He changes our hearts. His power, through hearts of gratitude and focused minds on Him, releases the grip our struggles have over us. We're strengthened by His peace, refuelled by His joy.

God's Word is filled with many reminders of how powerful and vital a thankful heart can be in this world.

It's not always easy to give thanks, but this is the very thing we must do in order to see God's will accomplished in our lives. This is how we move into higher realms of faith for ourselves, for our city, and for our nation. When we give thanks in the midst of difficulty, we bring pleasure to God's heart and breakthrough begins. He is looking for people who live in a realm of praise and thanksgiving where the enemy no longer has an ability to hold or manipulate. Satan is defeated when we have a thankful heart because thankfulness during difficulty is a sacrifice pleasing to God.

- Are you thankful?
- Are you thankful for your present circumstances?
- Are you thankful for your salvation, your friendships, and your job?
- Are you thankful for the way God made you?

Gratitude says a great deal about our character. It is the key that turns your situation around because it changes you, your outlook, and your attitude. There is power in a thankful heart. Thanksgiving brings contentment. An attitude of thanksgiving accepts and embraces God's will. Begin to thank God for all the blessings he has given instead of dwelling on the negative. Discontent dries up the soul.

Through Jesus, therefore, let us continually offer to God a sacrifice of praise—the fruit of lips that confess His name. (Hebrews 13:15)

To love God is to love His will. It is to wait quietly for life to be measured by one who knows us through and through. It is to be content with His timing and His wise apportionment. It is to follow in the steps of the Master, as did Paul, who was able to say that he had learned contentment no matter what the circumstances. His circumstances when he wrote that? Prison. No easy lesson, but great gain, which is the sum of godliness plus contentment. (1 Timothy 6:6)

Character is doing the right thing even when it costs more than you want to pay.

Michael Josephson

PART V

GOD ANSWERS PRAYERS

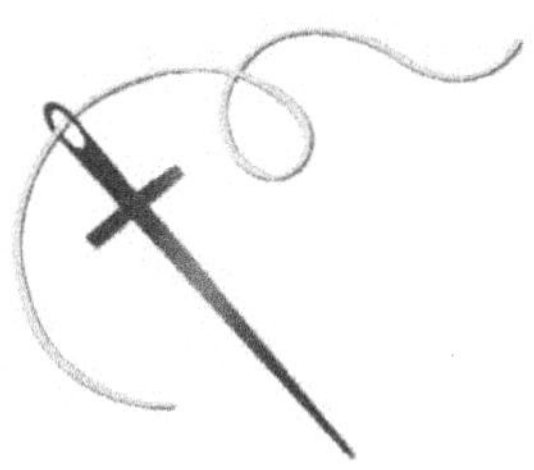

There is surely a future hope for you, And your hope will not be cut off.

Proverbs 23:18

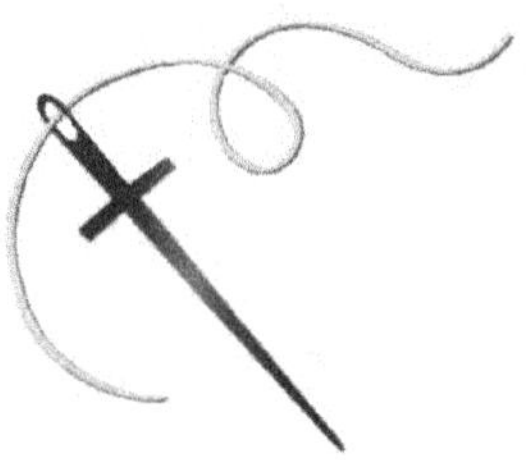

Character is higher than intellect.

Ralph Waldo Emerson

OWN YOUR FUTURE

"For I know the plans I have for you," declares the Lord, "plans to prosper you and not to harm you, plans to give you hope and a future.
Jeremiah 29:11

T he Bible provides us with a glimpse into the life of a man called Jabez, who saw himself differently from the way others saw him. He recognized that cultural and social limitations were not restricting his thinking and asked God to bless him:

And Jabez called on the God of Israel saying, "Oh, that You would bless me indeed, and enlarge my [a]territory, that Your hand would be with me, and that You would keep me from evil, that I may not cause pain!" So God granted him what he requested.
1 Chronicles 4:10

In seeking practical application for this verse, I considered the fact that many people are restricted from progressing in life because of small thinking or feel stuck in a particular station because of circumstances beyond their control. People struggling to get a break in life or facing discouraging moments need God to divinely enlarge their intellectual capacity to think beyond their limitations.

I believe the prayer of Jabez was a request for God to help him think differently, outside the proverbial box, so that he could live a blessed life. And, you know, that is exactly what God did.

God is always speaking, but are you capturing His thoughts? Are you disciplined enough to hear what He is conveying to you? Just as prayer, fasting, Bible study and worship keep us attuned to God's voice, procuring a vision for your life is a spiritual discipline that keeps you in sync with God's will for your life. Your future is His gift to you!

HOPE WHEN YOU HAVE UNANSWERED QUESTIONS

I am up early this morning. The grass is still wet from sprinklers, the birds just starting to greet each other for the day, and the sun is gently blowing the clouds out of the way so it can warm the earth. I love the quiet of this time but my mind is loud and crowded with concerns and worries.

I ask questions that I imagine you're asking too. What's going to happen? How long will this pandemic last? What does the future hold? I don't know the answers and God seems silent this morning. So I do the only thing I can: take one step forward, then another, and another. I pray as I do—messy, frustrated, confused prayers.

I think of one of my favourite Psalms, one I'd just reread in bed that morning.

"Why am I discouraged? Why is my heart so sad? I will put my hope in God! I will praise him again—my Saviour and my God!"
Psalm 42:5.

Can you relate to those words too? I'd not looked at this Psalm in a while and I became curious about how it ends. I was surprised to find the last verse is exactly the same as the one above,

"Why am I discouraged? Why is my heart so sad? I will put my hope in God! I will praise him again—my Saviour and my God!"
Psalm 42:11

I expected a neat bow tied around a truth, a restoration of confidence and certainty, a revelation that now everything would be different. But, no, the Psalmist still had the same questions. This is comforting to me right now in a season where so many questions don't seem to have answers. It's helpful to know that uncertainty doesn't equal a lack of faith or trust.

Yes, it is a fact that uncertainty doesn't equal a lack of faith or trust. What does the Psalmist do in the face of unanswered questions? He makes a choice: *"I will put my hope in God…I will praise Him again."*

One of the hardest parts of not knowing what's ahead is that it makes us feel powerless. But that's only an illusion. We can still choose our response.

The last seven or months have been extremely trying. However, imagine if you wrote a note that simply says, "God is in control, and I am in charge." Would anything get you down then? Most probably not.

That is what we need to know when life is uncertain. God is still in control. He has not forgotten us. We have not been abandoned. He is with us, for us, working on our behalf even now. We can trust Him no matter what happens. He has also given us stewardship of our everyday lives—what we do with our energy and emotions, resources and relationships. We are not helpless.

"I trust in your unfailing love"

Psalm 13:5

GOD CARES

We can all ask ourselves like the Psalmist, "What will I do today?" And know that whatever we choose to do, we are not alone for He has promised us, "And surely I am with you always, to the very end of the age."
Matthew 28:20

"How are you?" I ask (and really want to know).
"Oh, I'm so blessed!" she says, but the words feel forced.
I ask again, "I mean how are you, really?"
Her voice softens, "I'm ready to be done with all of this. It's harder than I thought it would be."

So which answer was true? Both.

We're funny as humans. We tend to think in terms of all or nothing, so we insist that life is great when we're breaking apart inside. Because to do otherwise would be to discount all of God's goodness in our lives, right? Nope, we always live with both blessings and brokenness. Challenges and victories. Sorrow and joy. They're all mixed up together.

Acknowledging the hard parts of our lives doesn't mean that we're not grateful for the gifts God has given. We can thank Him for the child He's given us while also feeling exhausted when that same child gets on our last nerve. We can feel deep appreciation for the job He's provided us with while wanting to beat our heads against our desks in frustration several times a day. We can wonder at how many blessings fill our lives while at the same time sensing an aching emptiness that comes from desires unfulfilled.

God understands both.

So what do we do? We embrace the paradox. We bring our sorrows as well as our joys to God. We say, "Thank You for this job. Please help me because it's wearing me out."

We pray, "Thank You for this child. Please give me strength because I feel like letting him join a traveling circus."

We declare, "Thank You for the blessings in my life. Please grant the desire of my heart that feels like a hole in the middle of all this wonderfulness."

What does it tell God when we do that? It says that we trust Him. Like the psalmist says,

"I trust in your unfailing love"
Psalm 13:5

In other words, "No matter what my circumstances are, I believe that You love me. And I will choose to recognize Your love in both the hard and happy parts of my life. I know I'm safe with You and I can bring everything about my experience on this earth to You."
He wants to know how you're really doing today.
And it's okay to tell Him.
All of it.

WHATEVER YOU ARE FEELING IS OKAY

But the fruit of the Spirit is love, joy, peace, longsuffering, kindness, goodness, faithfulness, gentleness, self-control. Against such there is no law.
Galatians 5:22-23

We've all been through a lot during the year 2020. Hard news. Cancelled plans. Social distancing.

I've heard people share how they're doing and then say, "But I shouldn't feel this way..." I want to remind us that whatever we're feeling today is okay. We're created with emotions for a purpose.

Fear and anxiety are protective emotions. They help us stay alert and pay attention, so having them right now is healthy and appropriate. We need to manage them, yes, but we don't have to make ourselves never experience them. When God says, "Do not fear" it's almost always to someone who's already afraid. It's not a rebuke, it's a reassurance and gentle invitation to trust Him.

Anger and frustration are informative emotions. We experience them when something important to us is threatened or a goal is blocked, revealing our values and desires. Graduation or wedding cancelled?

Anger is appropriate. Can't find food for your family at the grocery store? Expect to be frustrated. God doesn't tell us to not get angry, only to not let our anger lead us into unwise words or actions.

Grief and disappointment are adaptive emotions. We're all experiencing losses right now, some small, some huge. They all matter, so let's not dismiss any of them as insignificant or compare. Grief and disappointment tell us, "Things are not as I hoped they'd be."

These emotions can help us adjust to a new normal, draw closer to others, and eventually start moving toward new hopes.

Joy and happiness are sustaining emotions. It can be easy to feel guilty when we have happy moments at a time when so much is hard. But these emotions let us catch our breath, keep our hearts open, and energize us so we can keep going and help others. We also don't have to force ourselves to feel these emotions, they'll come eventually.

Emotions aren't the enemy; they're temporary messengers telling us about what we're experiencing. When one shows up, we can pause and ask,

- what is this emotion telling me?
- is it true?
- now what will I choose to do?

In the weeks and months ahead, we'll have many different feelings stop by for a visit. When one comes, we don't have to say, "I shouldn't feel this way."

All of our emotions are allowed. None of them are bad. As long as we remember that God is in control. In the Bible, Jesus demonstrates the full range of human emotions and expresses them in perfect love.

"How are you?" I ask and you answer, without thinking, "I'm fine."
It's the answer we all give. Often what we really mean is, "I'm a little tired. A bit overwhelmed. Longing for something more." In this world, our hearts grow weary. We want hope, joy, peace, and purpose. Surely all of this is around the next corner, we tell ourselves. If we hurry, if we try hard enough, then we'll find it.

On some mornings don't you want to just curl up under a blanket that feels like the edge of a cloud? Maybe turn on the lamp by your bed and sip a cup of sweet tea? You don't want this day to be like so many before. You want to know the answer to the restlessness in your heart. You need a real solution.

You considered calling your brother, maybe your older sister…no, maybe not. Then you reached for your Bible then and flipped through the pages. You began to notice verses about who God is and how He loves us. And suddenly came to a turning point. You realized what your heart needed wasn't a simple answer to a problem. No, you were looking for, longing for, a Person. We all are.

Someone bigger than us. Stronger. Able to handle everything. Someone who will care for us, fight on our behalf, and extend grace to us always. Someone limitless and loving, beyond our imagination, and right there in the intimate details of our lives—always the same and yet forever doing a new thing in and through us.

The God who scattered stars like diamonds across the velvet of the universe, the keeper of every sparrow, the maker of us all is inviting us to draw closer to Him. He is the place where our hearts can go on the hard days and the happy ones, in the highs and lows, when we are sad or frustrated or downright giddy. He is what we have been searching for all along. We don't have to settle for "I'm fine." Someone is whispering to us, inviting us, showing us in every moment, "I am God. I love you. You are mine."

HE WILL GRANT YOU THE DESIRES OF YOUR HEART

Delight yourself also in the Lord, and He shall give you the desires o your heart.
Psalm 37:4

This is a poem written by a teenage girl asking for a Godly husband. It was written as a prayer. This is what she said:

Dear God, I pray all unafraid
As girls are wont to be
I do not want a handsome man
But make him, Lord, like Thee.

I do not need one big and strong
nor yet so very tall,
Nor need he be some genius
or wealthy, Lord, at all;

But let his head be high, dear God,
and let his eye be clear,
His shoulders straight, whate'er his fate
whate'er his earthly sphere.

And let his face have character,
a ruggedness of soul,

And let his whole life show, dear God,
a singleness of goal.

And when he comes
as he will come
With quiet eyes aglow
I'll know, dear Lord,
That he's the man
I prayed for long ago.

That girl's name was Ruth Bell, and she later met and married Billy
Graham.

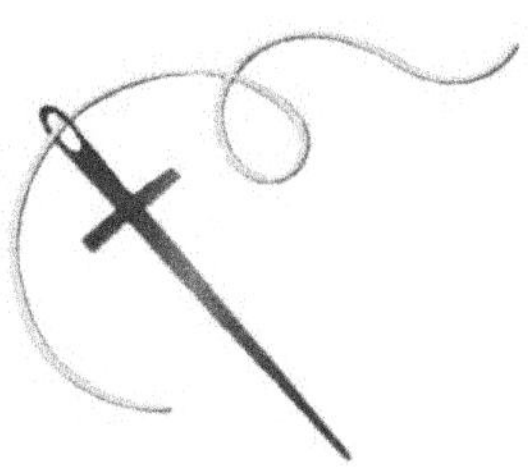

Fame is a vapor, popularity an accident, and riches take wings. Only one thing endures and that is character.

Horace Greeley

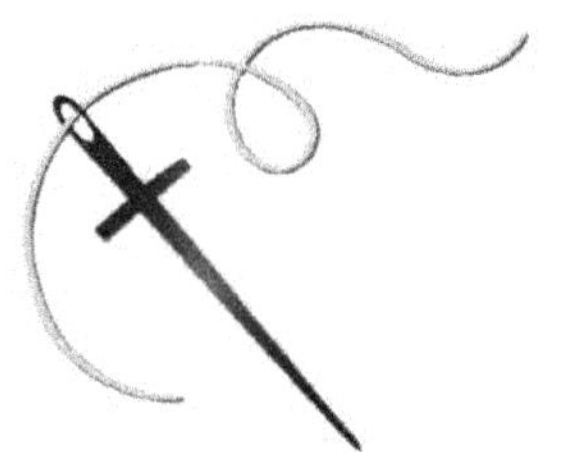

PART VI

TRUST IN GOD

What a gift life is to those who stay the course! You've heard, of course, of Job's staying power, and you know how God brought it all together for him at the end. That's because God cares, cares right down to the last detail."

James 5:11

All men are alike in their lower natures; it is in their higher characters that they differ.

John Christian Bovee

GOD KNOWS THE END OF THE STORY

Only I can tell you the future before it ever happens. Everything I plan will come to pass, for I do whatever I wish.
Isaiah 46:10

The big question everyone is asking right now is, "When will things get back to normal?"

But, I want to ask you, what will you do if life doesn't get back to normal?

The answer is simple. You don't put your hope in the government to make things right again. You don't trust in the media or celebrities. Instead, put your hope in God.

Why hope in God?

Because He knows the end of the story. We don't have to know it because He does. He holds the future.

The story of Job demonstrates this. Imagine being Job when everything was taken from him. He didn't know the future. He had no idea God would restore things in the end. But he trusted God.

James says,
"What a gift life is to those who stay the course! You've heard, of course, of Job's staying power, and you know how God brought it all together for him at the end. That's because God cares, cares right down to the last detail"
James 5:11

God worked through the details of Job's life because he cared about him. God will do the same for you. It doesn't matter how much you've messed up in the first part of your story; trust God to handle the details and watch how he brings it all together in the second half of your story. In fact, God already knows how your story will end.

The thing is, it's really His story and he created you to be a unique and significant part of it. That's why you can have faith that He is working to take care of you and to give you a good future.

God repeatedly says in Scripture that He will one day reward us for our faith. The book of James says:

"Happy are those who remain faithful under trials, because when they succeed in passing such a test, they will receive as their reward the life which God has promised to those who love him".
James 1:12

No matter what you're going through right now, God promises to work everything out for good. And that's a reason for hope—and a reason to faithfully trust in Him.

And the Lord answered me: "Write the vision; make it plain on tablets,
so he may run who reads it.

Habakkuk 2:2

SETTING THE RIGHT COURSE

Commit to the Lord whatever you do, and he will establish your plans.
Proverbs 16:3

It is important to set the right course and if necessary, correct your course should you find you veered off-course as will happen from time to time in life.

There is a book by Richard Paul Evans entitled *The Broken Road*. It's about a man who mid-career, despite great material success, wonders if he has wasted his lie pursuing the wrong goals. It is a story of second chances. It got me thinking what a terrible thing it is to live with regret but an even worse thing to die with it.

The author of *The 7 Habits of Highly Effective People*, Stephen R. Covey, warns against working *"harder and harder at climbing the ladder of success only to discover it's leaning against the wrong wall"*.

Too many people come to the end of their lives with misgivings or disappointment, or to the end of the road, only to find that they were on the wrong road all along. These people failed to begin with the end in mind. They neglected to look ahead and identify where they hoped to go, let alone design a roadmap to get there.

It is critical that we deliberately pursue a meaningful vision, become clear on the nature of our truest desires, and intentionally set a course to fulfil them. Allow God to fill our heart, mind and soul with a vision.
Vision takes you to a land called tomorrow if it is divinely inspired.

OWN YOUR DREAM

…the Lord was with (Joseph) and that the Lord made all he did to prosper in his hand.
Genesis 39:3

Success can never be measured by bank balances. Money measures only prosperity. Success is a matter of character.
Author Unknown

Remember the story of Joseph, the dreamer, and great grandson of Abraham, the great patriarch of faith?

When he went to work for Potiphar as a field hand on his estate, it was not long before he was running the place. Was he still a servant? Yes. Potiphar was in charge but he was an army general and not a farmer or estate manager. He was good at winning battles not at growing crops, storing them and getting them to the market.

If Joseph had only done what Potiphar directed him to do, Potiphar's estate would have been no better than before. However, under Joseph's hand, his assets multiplied like never before. How did this happen? Because Joseph knew how to tap into his divine genius to serve his master. He had a gift for learning and administration.

Sometimes you need to see beyond what people are ask you to do because most people don't know what it is they want, let alone how to get it. Take ownership of your own divine destiny and be strategic about bringing it to pass. It is up to you to understand, initiate and purposefully pursue your greater potential. Think of the future God has imagined for you and work towards it to make sure you measure up in the end. God sees your identity in Christ and the authority He's given you in His name - the world's "hope and glory" Colossians 1:27. Own your divine destiny and make a difference in the world, for His glory!

MEETING THE PERSON YOU ARE DESTINED TO BE

With God all things are possible.
Matthew 19:26

Each new day you are given an opportunity to close the gap between who you are dreaming of becoming and what you are destined to do. You have created that dynamic tension between what is and what could be that will energize your focus and pull you forward. The clearer the vision you have of what is most attractive about the other version of you, the stronger that pull will be.

Imagine for a moment, what it will be like when God introduces you to the person He had hoped you would become, the version that walks in the fullness of the identity and authority He called you up to be in Christ? We carry so much potential, especially those of us who have inherited "the promises that enable us to share in His divine nature" (2 Peter 1:4)

I believe the comfortable road will never lead you to the person you were destined to be in your life. The point is, your new frontier is just beyond your comfort zone. If you are too comfortable where you are right now you are probably not engaged in chasing that person that you could become. You are not running the race to win the race set before you (1 Corinthians 9:24)

Only when you are in hot pursuit of the best version of yourself are you making good on the promise God created you to share with your life. You carry the seeds of solutions, the missing pieces of a puzzle, and the answers to someone's prayer simply by faithfully stewarding the dreams and desires God has deposited in your heart.

The trouble is, rather than actually living the life we are destined to live, most of us settle for something close to that life. We allow ourselves to live in the shadow of what we were meant to accomplish without actually achieving it. We give in to the fear of stepping out toward that new frontier and settle instead for something that feels closer to home but is much less meaningful to the world around us and to ourselves. We accept life in the shadows rather than stepping out into the light of where we were really meant to live.

So today, make the commitment, ask the Holy Spirit for guidance and then boldly step out into the fullness of whatever it is that He guides you to be. Your mind - your imagination – is your greatest asset. As Napoleon Hill famously put it, "Whatever your mind can conceive and believe, it can achieve." Whatever you focus your mind on will prosper.

What are you going to focus on?
Take action. In fact, take the initiative to ignite your divine genius by calling out to the person you can be, doing the things you have been uniquely wired to do, and accomplishing the goals you are gifted to achieve. Position yourself today to make the most of tomorrow's

promise. Imagine who you will become in the days, months and years ahead.

Above all, keep in mind,
"With God all things are possible." Matthew 19:26

I have discovered that we may be in some degree whatever character we choose. Besides, practice forms a man to anything.

James Boswell

MY PRAYER FOR YOU

I succeed by attracting to myself the virtues, forces, and resources I wish to use, and I invite other people who work with me to do the same.
2 Peter 1:2-10

Today marks a new chapter of an amazing story yet to be told. You get to confer with God in deciding the theme, the players and the outcomes of the rest of your life. He will empower you to write your own story on the pages of your life. Make it noteworthy. Make it impossible to be ignored. Make it epic.

I pray that you will give life all you've got and then some. That you will commit to an action that moves you closer to your dreams. May you live such a life that if it were a book, you would be a best seller. Live passionately, live fearlessly and live boldly. Live your one precious life with no regrets.

May your guiding principles for life and living be biblically based, values driven, socially impactful, inter-culturally appealing and relevant to the times in which you live (Isaiah 58:12)

May your heart always be filled with gratitude and peace, not as the world gives peace but only as the Lamb of God can and has done.

Boldly declare the truth about your life from God's Word as you walk confidently towards your destiny:

"…but this one thing I do, forgetting those things which are behind and reaching forward to those things which are ahead, I press toward the goal for the prize of the high calling of God in Christ Jesus."
Philippians 3:13-14

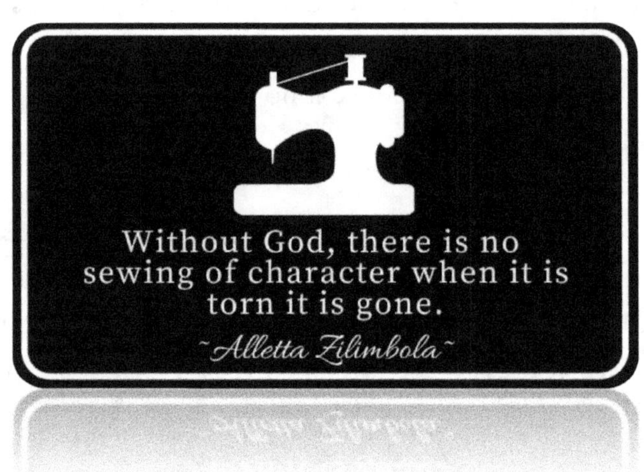

DECLARATIONS

Today I will set my priorities and focus on the things that really matter (Matt. 6:33)

I walk in forgiveness toward others and myself (Col. 3:13)

I declare peace within my mind and my relationships (Ps. 119:165; John 14:27; 2 Cor. 13:11)

I live, walk, and conduct my life by faith (2 Cor. 5:7; Heb. 10:38)

I realize I cannot embrace what You have for me in my future until I let go of my past (Phil.3:13-14)

I know my mind-set determines my progress and success, so today I choose to think on whatever things are true, honest, just, pure, lovely, and of good report; if there is any virtue and anything praiseworthy, I think on those things. (Phil.4:8)

I communicate with honesty and act with integrity (Eph. 4:25)

I diligently love and care for my family (1 Tim. 5:8)